Life Lessons: Ruminations on Life as a Human on Earth

Life Lessons: Ruminations on Life as a Human on Earth

ESSAYS BY MARY A FADERAN, PHD

• • •

Mary A Faderan, PhD

© 2017 Mary A Faderan, PhD
All rights reserved.

ISBN: 0692960635
ISBN 13: 9780692960639

Table of Contents

Introduction vii

Contemplation 1
The Great Divide.. 5
The Final Question.. 9
When it is Time to Quit... 13
Ruminations of Life as a Scientist................................ 17
How to Give The Most Impressive Presentations 23
How to Make an Exit Strategy...................................... 29
How to Cope with Multiple Projects on Your Plate.................. 35
How to Cope with Stress on the Job................................ 41
The Gift of Years... 47
How to be a Team Player 51
Finessing the Transition to Manager: Advice from the
Perspective of Direct Reports 55
How to Decide if You Ought to Jump Ship 59
Life Lessons from the Corporate World 63
The Frog in Hot Water – Is that You? 67
What are Some of the Advantages and Disadvantages of
Using Social Media to Get a Job After College?................... 71
Independence 79
Happiness 83
Last Things... 87

My Rant on the Closing of Our Marsh Store 89
The Dream 95
The Learning 99
The Lesson I Learned 103
The Lie 107
The Nurturing 111
The Object in My Junk Drawer 117
The Separator 119

Introduction

• • •

My book is about taking a journey with me through life's lessons. I've been in many types of work environments throughout my years. From being a lab receptionist while I was going to college, to being a postdoc at Yale, to being a regulatory scientist at a big private medical device company. In each phase of my life, I've been blessed to take note of how people are like, appreciated many who have helped as mentors, found and discovered different personality types, become more or less self-sufficient in dealing with issues that come up either in the workplace or in my private life. What comes up time and time again is, that God has been keeping tabs on me, and I have been giving Him all of what I'm going through. It's a regular communication and sometimes (most of the time) I am faithfully sending these thoughts to him and I don't get anything in return. Yet, throughout the years, and in the way events have happened in my life, there is an unmistakable message that keeps coming back to me: I am with you. So that is what this book is about. It's about how to deal with lessons from life, how to cope with being the pawn of a great corporate entity, how to deal with success, how to retrieve the lost idealism of life, and how to find the love that was there at the start. My book is also about how to give God His due, your attention and your prayers in all phases of life. God is always there.

Some of those who read this may feel uneasy about talking to God. But there are days when He is ALL you can really talk to. There won't be anyone, anybody, that will be the answer to all your prayers, except God Almighty.

My hope is that those who read this book will gain encouragement and hope, and perhaps find solutions as well.

West Lafayette, Indiana
September 27, 2017

Contemplation

• • •

THERE HAVE BEEN MANY BOOKS written by holy people about contemplation. I recall reading Thomas Merton's book Seeds of New Contemplation, which I don't remember much of, but I do recall that he really was very introspective, and gave a good argument to contemplation.

What is contemplation? It can be many things. One can just sit back and pause in the day's work and contemplate things - turn over a problem in one's mind, or appreciate what the day is like. In my thoughts, I think contemplation is more of a way to see what life is really all about. What is my life about? Is there purpose to it? Is it going where it ought to be? Where can I right the wrongs I've done? Who else can I reach out to to make things happen, to make things right, to get to where I want to go?

Contemplation is a good thing. Like vitamins every day. It makes the soul, the psyche, find its moorings. It makes life happy. It removes the humdrum from the day. Contemplation is not frequently found in people who are always attached to their cell phones, whipping them out at every buzz that they feel in their back pockets. Contemplation is not something a lot of people do these days. There's always distractions - doesn't matter what they are, they are distractions and one must flee to a place somewhere within to get to contemplate.

So is contemplation like praying? Well, it can be. I think praying is the act of invoking God to come and listen to you and help in your decisions. I think that praying is a part of contemplation. But contemplation is something that gives you the path to prayer. There needs to be a way to get to contemplating what is there out there, what lies ahead, what is really there and what is all illusion.

Life is full of illusions, as you might guess. There's illusions like "You need to go to X and X schools to get the best jobs" or, "You MUST buy this product or vehicle or house to be recognized as someone with stature." Illusions are everywhere. And contemplation clears off the dust of illusions and makes things more immediate to your attention. If you contemplate, for example, your marriage - who did you marry and why is that person your spouse? Did you marry them to get status? Did you give up someone else that you love to marry this spouse to get somewhere you THOUGHT was where you wanted to be? That sort of thing. You might even think about (and thinking is a big part of contemplation) what you might change if you only had some way to get change. You all want to change something, somehow. You all wish to make life better. To find a peace that transcends all knowing.

Peace is the key.

Contemplation is the KEY to peace. It is where all the unhappy, niggling thoughts get put into their slots and then locked away deep into the netherworld. Never to bother you again. Because each thought is captured and made into an argument, and then when you win the argument (with the right thought) then that niggling bothersome thought will go away and find a place away from you. It won't come back.

It is really important that every person still alive to think of contemplation. It is all encompassing. It involves thought, prayer and peace as the outcome. It can be peaceful already when you contemplate because the psyche is being given attention. And the Psyche knows and it quells all other distractions. It must be given time, space and the energy that is positive.

What is most important is that part of contemplation where you need to ask Who you must have in your thoughts to solve and change and become free. That Who is your Creator. The One who called you into being. Who called you to Contemplate His Goodness. Who gave you life. And a mind. And a body with which to do things.

Image copyright: Copyright: <a href='https://www.123rf.com/profile_lenanet'>lenanet / 123RF Stock Photo</a>

The Great Divide

• • •

I WENT TO SHOP AT Target the other day. I had a free afternoon, and was perishing to have a drink of cold iced tea. I stood with my cart in line to get waited on. There were two women in front of me. Instead of whipping out my cell to check the latest on Instagram, I looked about. In that instant, I had the long line of vision of two workers who stood, several yards from me and from each other. The first worker was a man, someone who worked in the deli. He was putting in some newly made deli sandwiches. The woman was at the end of my line of vision, she stood in the bakery section. She looked as though she was weary, passing her hands over her face. And then i realized she was laughing at someone's conversation - that someone was out of my view.

I felt a slight inclination to study them. They were ordinary people, they were not anyone that would really catch anyone's attention. But the ordinariness of their posture, the routine-ness of their jobs, the way the woman stood somewhat unoccupied taking a break to chat - the scenes were arresting. I started to think about them and all those like them. Who are they? What are they like? Do they like their jobs? Would they want to find a better place to work? Is it a good place where they are? Why did they take these jobs over others? Is it something that they had to have to keep from going downhill? Is there a way for them to move forward - upward or laterally? Why would they want to just be like what they are now? Would they?

I know that the economy is built on people - workers - such as these. Such as us working stiffs. They are the ones that make the workday hum with activity. Or are they? I think that maybe We the customers make their world hum. If there weren't people like us, they would be doing things in vain, a futile work. Yet, for all it looks, the store is humming along. There are lines to the registers. There are people browsing. I enjoyed the Starbucks ice tea, and I strolled along the well-arranged aisles while sipping it.

But I wonder whether all employees of all businesses are content with what they have, what they are there and how they are seen. Is it easier for someone in retail, for example, to move around and be happy with their peers? Is it less stressful on the psyche to be baking, slicing deli meat, ringing up groceries, hanging up clothes than paper pushing, scrolling through Excel spreadsheets and attending meetings? What would one give up for the job in the other side of the business fence? Would I have been better at retail than in a corporate environment? Is there really a great divide? Yes, of course, there's more at stake in the corporate environment, the salaries are large and yet - it's a very high stress job to be in that milieu.

For me, I've been in both. I worked in retail for a span of months, while waiting for the right job. I wasn't proud to go into retail. I must say that I didn't like it much. I wanted what I thought was a bigger salary, a lot more responsibilities, and a better health insurance. But, for those who stay in that milieu, I really feel that perhaps that would have been more like a walk in the park, compared to being on the hook for a big project. Fast forward to a few years ago. Those questions would have been answered by me as - yes, I'll slice the deli meat over meeting with the big cheese. Deli meat slicers aren't intimidating. The "big cheese" are.

There are pluses and minuses here that I enumerate. It's really up to those who still work whether they want to do one or the other. Of course, the business milieu needs more education, and that might be why many remain in retail. There just isn't a pathway that might be available to them. But must business/corporate life be the ONLY path forward? I suggest to those who are wishing to breach the fence - don't just go for the money. Go for what the next job will fulfill in your life: a family, a good home, time to spend broadening horizons, education, and a peace that surpasses all knowing.

Image copyright: <a href='https://www.123rf.com/profile_3dagentur'>3dagentur / 123RF Stock Photo</a>

The Final Question

• • •

JUST A WHILE AGO, A wealthy man asked me to answer a question: I have everything – I have money, prestige, power, great kids, everything that I ever worked for. I worked hard for it. I have it all. But I don't have what I really want. I don't have someone. I can't find that someone. I thought I lost her. I thought I never had her. I don't know whether I ever did have someone. It seemed like she wasn't real, this person I was wanting. Now, I feel like I don't have ANYTHING. There ain't nobody to be sharing all this good God given wealth with. Do I try to find that someone when I have so much already? Is this enough? What do I look forward to? I can't deal with it. I feel like I won at something but lost something bigger.

I don't have a good answer for this question. I think though, that this man should first of all ask God that question. God reads our hearts. He knows before we even know it. That would be my first response. The second thing is – start from where you were in the beginning. See where it all went south. Find out who was there in the beginning. Was that person the right one? Did you and she share the same dreams? And were these dreams good? Did you both want to do good things for others? Help others together? Were you thinking of telling the other your plans? Or did you just find yourselves going apart? Did the money and prestige give you both other things to pursue separately?

The other thing I'd do now, after all is said and done, is to find what YOU want to do. Going after the thing that gives your heart a warm feeling. Most of the time, when you do this, when you pursue this kind of path – being good to those who need help, helping the poor, visiting the prisons, giving to a worthy and good cause, going back to the idealism of your youth, you will find that person. That person is going to be in the thick of it. You'll be able to tell. However, you will have to tread carefully. Think of all those times when you tried to elbow your way to the top of the crowd just to impress someone. This person will not be impressed by your wealth and prestige. This person won't be impressed by your looks, your dress, what you own. No, this person will say, He's got a lot of money, but he looks like he's too sure of himself and won't be giving of himself.

It's your own SELF that you need to give in order to receive the GRACE of love. If it is meant to be, love will return. Or find you. You have to ask God to see where you went wrong. Why you went for the money and not for love. Or why this or that instead of the other. Only you and God can really communicate with each other about your life and where it started and how it is now. The only thing I can say is that, in everything you do, ask God for help. He will find you the answer. And He will let YOU KNOW that the answer you want and need to find happiness IS WITH YOU.

Image copyright: <a href='https://www.123rf.com/profile_iqoncept'>iqoncept / 123RF Stock Photo</a>

If not now, when?

When it is Time to Quit

• • •

Now that I've told you all about how to make an exit strategy, test the waters and find your passion, I am going to tell you when it is time to quit. This post is more for my own edification and not anyone else's.

So you are quitting your job. You are leaving the place where you've been for the last umpteen years. I know I've told you before that you need to have place to go to. Well, there are times when you just have to leave and walk away. The waters where you live and work from 8-5 pm each day have gotten warmer and warmer. You are surrounded. Surrounded by whales and sharks and all sorts of marine life. Whales that push you to your limits. Sharks that make it so hard to concentrate because their teeth are on your back, making you seek healing each day – Tylenol, pain meds, even massage therapists. You feel as though there can't be any resolution but one thing – leaving.

I'm sure that you will find another job somewhere. A job that you can enjoy. Maybe you have a few more years to retirement. That will be welcome. Why not wait, you ask? You think that the call of retirement is getting louder. You like being at home with your furkids or your significant other or your grandkids. Working on whatever passion you have. Taking it to a higher level.

So you are now making a decision. To keep your job and die each day, or to leave and then LIVE as you wish to. The difference is in many things: money, money, money. You are not going to be earning anything for a few weeks, maybe months. You hope to find another job somewhere else. You need to take out money from savings and live on it for now. You have to sign up for insurance. You're navigating the waters of unemployment, self-willed unemployment, and finding out where the comfort zones are. You need to keep a log of what you're going through. Each day that passes, do you think you did the right thing by leaving? Are you poorer but happier? When does the balance turn completely in your favor? It's that outlook, that ability to focus forward and not inward nor backward that is most important. You have made a leap of faith. You are not drowning, you are treading water. But there is a pull to keep you from sinking. That pull, my friend, is God. He will lead you out of the desert, out of the pit, out of that dark cave where you dwelt with monsters and <u>He will make it all new for you</u>.

Image copyright: <a href='https://www.123rf.com/profile_convisum'>convisum / 123RF Stock Photo</a>

Ruminations of Life as a Scientist

• • •

As I've been writing about the corporate life, I don't want to exclude other types of "work environments" out there. I've worked in different workplaces, hospitals, labs and research institutions.

I think that working in labs can be a drudgery. That can be a killer. I have been in research and in that milieu, the research staff that I've worked with have been very well mannered. I think that I was lucky to have had good experiences in research labs. I understand that in that sort of environment, ambition is still up there in the goals, but, it is a common goal for all involved that the research mission is important and must always be kept in mind when carrying out experiments.

In one workplace I've been fortunate to work in, I was in NYC, and was at the lab of a famous Cancer research professor and doctor. He was prolific in his interests and research. Many people from around the world came to his lab to get experience and find a key focus to work on when they went back to their home countries and strike out on their own. I met many foreign nationals there, and made good friends with them. The technicians were also good and hard working. It is a very good blessing for a research director to have good techs that work for him. These are the backbone of a good lab. Without those techs, the lab would fall apart. Post-docs (as I used to be) will come and go, and there is turnover which for some people is an unstable way of life. Like those who practice medicine, post-docs search high and low for a good lab to get published and get recognized and hope to land a high paying job in industry. Academia is the one place that many post-docs go but that is another place where the "publish or perish" meme exists. This is a hard life for those who struggle already at the post doc level. For those who feel that they can pursue a lasting research, then academia is where they should thrive. There are so many minefields there though – things like having to kowtow to the chair of the department, having to keep going to conferences even to the other side of the world, having to publish in good and excellent journals, having to pursue funding from all over the place. The one place that I was happy to find funding for my post doc was from the government (NRSA). It afforded me the opportunity to work at an Ivy League school.

But, I digress.

The thing that I find disparate between corporate and academic life or industry and academia, is that in industry, the main goal is something that one may or may not wish to really work on. If one is in love with the study of amoebic life, but works for a pharmaceutical company then the separation from that company is pretty clear. The main goal of industry is to get the main product pipelines to market. In academia, the purpose of research is to find something that's new and interesting and may (read: may) have relevance to science in general. So when I was in my first job after grad school, the one "flavorite" topic people were talking about was "ubiquitin" and I felt that I had no real interest in it, but it appeared in many papers and people got famous because of it. Nowadays, I don't know much about the newest and greatest in science and research, but at least as far as I know research is still flourishing.

One problem I see however, is that PhDs that are being generated these days end up working for places in a temporary job. There are way too many PhDs coming out of grad school and they seem not to have a really good idea where they want to end up.

These are all my opinions and there isn't evidence that's there I can quote. But these are my impressions.

The one other thing I think is missing in corporate but not in academia, is the camaraderie that exists in labs, especially in labs where the principal investigator is willing to nurture and teach his or her teams. There were many times when we organized parties celebrating birthdays, Chinese New Year, and other holidays at the labs I worked at. There were after-hours gatherings at the nearest pubs and pizza places. Trips to the Met to listen to Placido and Pavarotti. One or two picnics and volleyball games. It is not all like that in corporate, and yet some corporations do their own ways of building up esprit de corps (like in-house gyms, picnics and annual parties). But a research lab is more of a close-knit bunch of people who share the great desire to discover big things in a group setting.

One time in NYC, my lab-mates and I decided to watch Shakespeare in the Park. I hiked with them from our First Avenue lab building and sat with our group waiting to hear whether we would get tickets to watch. We watched the rest of the people there playing football or enjoying the summer sun. Then, we heard we didn't get tickets and I was so mad and disappointed. Suddenly, the skies opened and buckets of rain came down all upon us. People fled to every direction. One of us apparently had a resourceful husband who came to take us in a cab and took me home to Queens, and them to their far Rockaway residence. I had a rather amusing time after all that thinking of all those who were given tickets to the Shakespeare play. Alas, my new Nike walking shoes never survived all the water they took in.

If you asked me now which one wins over the other, I would say that research is probably more interesting. One doesn't have to sit all day at a desk and do endless documents or Excel spreadsheets. At the lab, I walked or stood a lot and therefore used up energy, and was active. At the lab, there were many opportunities to listen to guest lecturers, attend group journal updates, and go to visit other labs in different universities to learn new techniques. It is a more fertile place to learn and grow as an intellectual. And even more important, it affords one more opportunities to get to know others in a more personal way. One of the places I worked as was where I met the one I fell in love with.

It's good to reminisce about the good things about working in academia. The only problem there of course, is that the pay isn't as good and there might be a risk of losing grants and therefore having to find another lab to work in. It's a part of life, and there are casualties in that area as well.

Image copyright:
<a href='https://www.123rf.com/profile_jannoon028'>jannoon028 / 123RF Stock Photo</a>

How to Give The Most Impressive Presentations

• • •

I RECENTLY HEARD A PRESENTATION from a colleague and decided that I should write about how to give a presentation that is lasting and impressive. Why would anyone want to have a lasting and impressive presentation? Well, it can really be lasting and impressive if it's pretty awful – people filing out of the room shaking their heads and muttering about how awful it was. But I wish to be positive. We all want to give a positive impression to those who are our peers, who judge our work, who value us as their employees, who make decisions on whether to approve or disapprove. It is important to make a good case for ourselves, for our project and for our continued employment.

I think that the first thing one needs to do is to make some preliminary notes as to what the presentation is all about. Find out who is necessary to be there to listen (don't need to invite people who might not care or won't matter), and what their positions are and how they might be able to help you in your presentation (at the time you make the presentation). Now, the meeting I went to had an extraneous person present. He did have the credentials to be there, he was knowledgeable about projects of this scope, but he had no real investment in the project. His job was to comment, if necessary, and to make a reassuring presence to the host of the presentation.

The next thing you need to do is to put together in an outline form what you intend to talk about. Is this about your project? Is it a sales pitch? Is it something that is needing the major players to discuss and decide? Sort of a Go-NoGo type of meeting. There other meetings too, like those where you plan with your team what needs to be accomplished in the next quarter. That is easier because you're more comfortable, the team is known to you, and they all want to help in meeting your goals and metrics. Not that the key meeting or presentation doesn't want you to succeed, but these are people who come from different departments. Such as – executive office (CEOs, management), marketing, quality (if you work for a manufacturer), engineering (if you work in production or manufacturing, or medical) and those who disseminate information (PR and communications). It may be all or not all of the above who will come. It really depends on what you wish to present, how you want these key people to react and ask questions that are meaningful to you.

The third thing you need to do is to put together your evidence – data, supporting figures, graphics, tables, other types of creative work that's been done so far. In the case where I was an observer and decision maker, it was all the above and more. Sometimes, you will have to decide that the data you will give is going to look dull and boring. It is a turn off, I admit, to give a slide that looks like a table with a lot of figures or characters. However, it behooves your listener and audience to take these as the meat and potatoes of your presentation. Why else are you presenting? If this is the case, and there are many things to discuss, you need to give them a capsule summary of what these figures all mean. If these people want to dwell on these don't go too fast and just let them digest. That is also key. I think people who hurry through slides have not the right attitude. It's rude to do this, and it won't help your cause in the long run.

PowerPoint has been around long enough and newer types of presentation software have also come around. One of them is called Prezi which is a quirky way to present ideas. It may be a bit hard to work with, as I've only seen it presented twice. I suggest that you work with the software presentation that works well with your materials and you can maneuver without having to think too much about it. You need to give the evidence straight, and not mess with graphic and twisted slides (figuratively).

There are those who criticize presenting straight from the slides. I don't know why they feel that reading from the slides is that bad. Many good organizational presentations are just like that. It isn't a sin, really. Only fools think that reading from the slide is bad form. I do know that if you insist of reading only the stuff you present, then it is going to be needing a bit more of your finesse. You need to comment on the figures and tell the significance, unless that is also on the slide. For those who tend to forget, put everything that's important on the slide. The take-away is needed and those who are more oriented to visuals will see that straightaway.

When you are already at the meeting, try to look more decent than your business casual. I have learned that when one presents one needs to dress a notch above the audience appearance. The meeting I was in was good – the speaker had a tie and jacket on, and probably went to have his hair cut and so on. When all are present, it is also good to have an assistant or team mate take notes that will be important in reviewing what everyone said and what action items are needed to be addressed.

Go through the presentation in a calm, unhurried way. One professor I listened to was quite good at it. He talked calmly, without emotion (but not boring), and gave an impression that his work was good without outwardly saying so. He was a professor from Oxford University (UK) and that was my role model for years in presenting. This style really also helps to calm yourself down.

When it comes to questions, don't be flustered if someone asks a question in the middle of your presentation. This is always the way I'm used to. It only means that they are interested and invested in your presentation. If you don't know the answer (which I hope isn't all the time), tell them you don't know but that you'll get back to them with the answer at a later time. They will not be indignant at this. Don't push your luck though because if you are unprepared that will be a very sad thing. So this means, you need to anticipate questions. This is good to do when you are finished writing your presentation and reviewing it for content. If they tell you something that corrects your work, don't be defensive – thank them and say that you appreciate their comment.

Anticipate, anticipate, anticipate questions. Don't think you're done just because the slides are all done. Ask someone to review them as well and find out what their take is on them. But try to think like your audience at their level. Be the CEO, be the production manager, be the communications editor, be the extraneous person there who has no real investment in the project but has a common goal to further the company's mission. See how they might ask you what is pressing on their minds.

Don't be sarcastic. Don't be insulting to those who ask. This is not really necessary for those who are in the know. You really can't be in a joking mood when you're addressing executives. I suppose some companies are that laid back, but you need to respect your audience even if they are known to be unpleasant people to deal with. Always give each your consideration, respect and good manners. It will be something that will last in their memory of you and your demeanor when you are kind and respectful always.

When things get testy, if the presentation creates some tension, it is good to say that this discussion needs to be offline and proceed from there. If people insist, tell them that you can't address it but that you will give it the full attention it needs after the meeting. If you must, have a glass of water with you to help you take a breather.

When there is a subset of the audience that take on their own conversation within your presentation, pause the meeting and inquire whether there was something you can help them with. It might be best to ask them there and then in order to stop the undervoice conversation, and bring the group to their attention. This helps to diminish the side convos. If they have anything to say, they will and if they were only being distracting, they will cease. It may work 80% of the time, and the other 20% you will just have to talk over them and not lose the meeting that way. This is something that's a peeve of mine but it's possible that this happens in all corporate meetings. I find this behavior unruly but that might just be me being schoolmarmish than anything else.

When everything has been discussed, the notebooks are shut, the slides are reading "The End", it is good form to thank everyone for their attention and the questions. Tell them that they will be welcome to read the minutes of the meeting or that these will be circulated for their signatures. If everyone is happy, they will smile and thank you for being so good.

After the meeting, kick back with a little refreshment and help yourself to lollygagging the rest of the day. Your work is done for that day and be a friend and help to the rest of your team. If this is a high stakes presentation, bring something from a bakery or high end pastry shop the next day to thank your team. You know what to do with that more than I – but thank your team for helping you. They will keep you happy that way.

Image copyright:
<a href='https://www.123rf.com/profile_andreypopov'>andreypopov / 123RF Stock Photo</a>

How to Make an Exit Strategy

• • •

THIS POST IS FOR THOSE guys and girls who are hating their jobs and can't figure a way out.

There are times in one's life when they figure they need to get out of their current circumstances. For corporate life, this is probably going to have a few things to include. First, do you want to go to another corporate environment? If you do, then consider whether you really want to deal with the same headaches that you have now. Do you want to move to a parallel position? Do you want to have a promotion to be manager there where you want to be? If you want the same level of work, be sure you can deal with the superiors there and the hiring manager. If you think that is good, and the environment has the right elements in it, then go for it. Same with the promotion at the other company. If you think you'll be a little out of your league with a new set of direct reports (having had none before) be very sure you can deal with them. The one thing I recommend is to create a checklist of what you like and hate about the current corporation you work in. Then, after you've taken a look at the new place and the culture there, figure out the differences and whether there's a favorable balance in favor of you moving over there.

One thing about exit strategies is, that you may really want to eschew Corporate life forever. Where would you go instead? Are you really going to be happy as a part of a cog or wheel? Do you care about the mission statement of the company or the one you want to go to? What is YOUR mission statement? Why not write that down somewhere and keep it safe. In fact, go back to it more than once and see whether it rings true when you do review it. Let some weeks go by and see if the statement is still You. What I wish for everyone to know is that working for a corporation is not that bad, if you are willing to be part of a team, if you like the work enough, if the supervisors give you latitude. But, if something isn't right with the company, if their work ethics aren't jiving with their mission statement or with yours, then figure out that maybe it's really time to WRITE your own exit strategy.

I can't write this for you, of course. Each one has to do this. Call it an exercise. A "What if" statement or goals. If this happens, what will you do?? If that happens, will you change course? It is going to be a long process, I think for each person to create this strategy. It will take some time, and let it simmer along. Just don't jump out so suddenly and then find out that you got into something worse or are at loose ends.

For the simmering process, you should let the weeks and months go by. Let your paychecks keep you stable. Let your eyes watch and ears hear. Make note (if you want to write it down somewhere in a safe place at your own place) about what is different, who is leaving and who is coming on board. See what the managers are saying. Look at the profit margins, look at how transparent the company is with the employees. Are they saying they are transparent but maybe they're not? Are they really saying the numbers are going up or are they doing something fancy with the math?

It's a game, really. It's like you are the one that is watching the way the wind blows. See the ones who are staying and figure out WHY they stay. Or if they are really outrageous and do no work all day but talk about ridiculous stuff, then figure out WHY they HAVEN'T BEEN LET GO. These people, I must say, are NOT GOOD. They are serving a purpose for someone bad, someone who wants them to keep up with the cheer and talk but really siphoning out information about others to the 'bad guys', or even the bad supervisors.

What about the bad supervisors? Look at the ones who are in management. Are they all good? Do they have a competence that keeps the company values going? Have they ever made anyone feel bad in front of others? Is their language good or are they just some people who happened to get into that job because they knew someone up in the levels. It is true there are many of these in many corporations. Have I totally demoralized you into leaving for a farm in Tennessee growing potatoes?

Well, there are many ways to leave, as I think, Paul Simon sang in his tune, 50 Ways.

What I think is nice is if you could have buy-in from your significant other that you plan on leaving sometime in the coming year. What ifs come into play. If you have no significant other, then you are pretty much all set. No one to really have to be responsible for, just yourself. You can really do whatever you want, really. Go for another degree in something YOU LIKE TO DO. Like go and learn a trade, learn a way to help others with their problems, go and create your own company. The Small Business Administration is the one way to get a business going. They give grants, or fund your mission and goals. It is one way to go and if you are eager to work hard for YOURSELF, then do it. DO. IT.

I have to address those who have families. It's true you really need to figure out how to do a good exit if you have a family to support. If you have little kids and a spouse, you just have to deal with the thought that you may need more time, more support, more income somehow to go out and do something that you want for yourself and your family. If your spouse works, then figure out how to keep body and soul together on that spousal income, while you work on finding a great place to be in.

For every dream you MUST PRAY TO GOD. He is the Lord of the Dream, and you are one of His creations. He dreamt you up into being. He is THE ONE AND ALL. You MUST PRAY anyway. There is no going it alone. No one can do what they want on their own, not even with their families. It is not that way at all. God, GOD, is in control in everything. You really can't go without God. Just try to find a way to talk to Him each day. I guarantee that God hears everyone, and He won't forget you. As long as you talk to Him every single day.

The last exit strategy, if I haven't mentioned it through the subtleties of my blog, is that if you really want to do great, you just have to work for God. God is the one who gives us all we have, doesn't He? He gives us our intellect, our five senses, our jobs, our paychecks, our good thoughts, our families, our loves, our hobbies, our talents, our homes, our pets, our running water, the lights that keep our house lit, the furnace working, the cars in good shape, the new car and the loan that you had to take out to get it. He has given all these to you and everyone else. Now, the one thing that needs to be said is that you must - MUST THANK GOD for each of these, and ASK HIM to protect these. He will. I am sure He will. Now fear is going to make you think that God couldn't possibly do all this because maybe you aren't so good or you cheat at cards or whatever. Well, if you can ask God to make you BETTER PERSON, then that will keep the furnace going and the kids fed and the car running. Just try talking to God. Ask Him to write your mission statement for you. Let Him use you as His instrument. This is a gift from God. Don't tell me I didn't warn you ☺

Image copyright:
<a href='https://www.123rf.com/profile_stnazkul'>stnazkul / 123RF Stock Photo</a>

How to Cope with Multiple Projects on Your Plate

• • •

MANY PROBLEMS THAT ONE ENCOUNTERS in the corporate world are the multiple projects one gets assigned. You can be a team member or a manager, and for managers, this might be old hat, but it's always nice to get a review of what might one think of when thinking about handling projects.

The main thing I've been told is to manage these by their due dates. In which case, you need to break it down by when they are due – or, if there are a lot of things in one project to manage, break it into workable parts. So that means each part is going to have a due date. If the project is something only you can do, that means that you give yourself the tasks that the project is all about – for example, in my field, I have to write dossiers for registering products. That means I should know where to find the items on this document, get those in place and put them into folders and make them presentable. The ultimate thing in that is that the document which is the written summary or specification or information is factual, honest and straightforward so that the reviewers are in great comprehension about what you want to tell them and don't need to rummage through piles of attachments to find them.

If the project needs more people to help with, or that you are part of a large team, then you need to get together with these people but not necessarily in one big meeting. When there is a kickoff meeting, which I think is a blessing to all involved, then the leader needs to spell out and assign what tasks are needed to get the project off the ground into the next phase. Once these tasks are doled out, then each member will know what to do and be prepared to handle the work and then report back after a period of time.

Give yourself time to regroup, take breaks, talk about it with your coworkers or team members, see if anything comes out of that. There's good thoughts in numbers for the Holy Spirit works in many people and they each can give a suggestion on how to work on a knotty problem - it maybe that you can schedule meetings to work on it but these can be cumbersome due to other people's agendas, and so you may want to schedule coffee meetings or informal meetings with these people or, some time visit them in their comfort zones so that there will be better moods with thoughts that can help the person figure out your question. Don't waste their time, make an appointment to see them if that is something they are worried about. Many managers mention that they hate being interrupted, and that question "Do you have a minute?" makes them irate. Someone I know mentions this with sarcastic fondness when he is at a meeting himself. So take time to ask if they want to spend a bit more time with you and schedule a meeting.

Some people may rely a lot on those deadlines but then there might be a deadline that you can't meet due to vacation days and so on that fall on these dates. So you may have to create an artificial deadline that includes the demands of those stakeholders that want to review the job and outcomes before sending it on to their superiors. Also, ask the stakeholders whether there are any blockout dates that they can't do so that you can include those in the timeline. Some engineering departments have the Gantt chart but as I'm not an engineer, it is something slightly out of my field of knowledge. However, I am sure that those who are visually oriented will enjoy the Gantt chart. I also like the Bullet Journal, which I've taken up and that keeps me up on what I should be doing daily. It isn't perfect but then nothing really is. You need to figure out what is good for you and your type of learning and personality. If you tend to be a little out of kilter, then maybe three different types of charts or schedules are needed. One for your office (or two) and then one for your home (to schedule personal stuff as well – kids soccer and so on).

Meetings:

Before meetings one must always have an agenda to send out in advance so that one keeps to it. Someone, mostly YOU, who needs to steer the meeting away from those who tend to bloviate and eat up the time.

Meetings tend to be more formal in my experience so it is not the best time to free associate with your peers and superiors. Mainly one must be prepared to answer any questions, have all the facts (at the most, say if things aren't all done, then say it — and don't hem and haw about it). Nobody ever died of telling like it is – at least nobody in a decent and upstanding company. But please, keep the language clean and DON'T DRESS ANYONE DOWN IN PUBLIC. That is NOT done.

The other thing about meetings is that there may be too many attendees at the time and they might just be wasting their time being there. So if their role is small at the present time, just meet them one on one and then catch up the group with what you have learned.

Make the meeting less than an hour unless this is a project with many moving parts in which case, keep the meeting to one hour at the most because the moving parts may have to have each a meeting to have. Long meetings are such bores and then people whip out their cell phones and tend to lose interest. That is also NOT DONE in a good meeting. Keep those cell phones OUT of the meetings. Of course, those in marketing will complain but really that is not something anyone tolerates because there is a loss of attention and then they will be at fault when the project goes awry.

The people who are in charge - those who are managers- will be grateful if they have all they need from you - meetings are meant to update, find a solution to a common goal and get the project moving. Get people to accept action items and if possible have them all at a point where they can get them accomplished before another meeting needs to take place.

When the meeting is over, provide all the members of the team a breakdown of the meeting minutes so that they all can refer to them when they need to at a later date, or, at the next meeting.

At the next meeting, have those points ready and review them briefly.

These are just some thoughts that I've gathered as a result of being in all types of meetings. Have a good rest of your workday! Cheers from the Marian Musings Gang.

Image copyright: <a href='https://www.123rf.com/profile_ismagilov'>ismagilov / 123RF Stock Photo</a>

How to Cope with Stress on the Job

• • •

I AM SOMETIMES ASKED ABOUT how I manage stress on the job. One thing I did (which I suppose many can't do) was to transfer to a different department. The stress levels may change if you decide to look into that. Of course, it's always good to 'figure out' what sort of work the others do at that new department and then see if you can actually handle that compared to the work you do where you are. In extreme cases, changing jobs may be one way to handle stress, but that will incur more stress levels due to "location, location, location"! If you have a way to find a job "WHERE YOU ARE" in town, that would be great. I suppose that means you need to figure out your job there and the pay and then see whether you can actually get along with those people. So perhaps that's not so great either.

If that's the case, where perhaps at this time it's not good to go somewhere else in your location, then I suggest a few things:

1. Delegate, delegate, delegate. If you have anyone below you in seniority, have them handle the small stuff. You are being paid to do your stuff at your level. Don't try to hog the work, it won't help. And, it won't look good if someone in your staff isn't doing anything. It makes THEM look like a nonentity.
2. Find some time to get a vacation. That's what you do get each year, so USE IT. And, if you don't care to travel, then DON'T TRAVEL. Vacations are too over-advertised where they entice

you to GO somewhere. Well dear, you will get EVEN MORE STRESS from traveling and all the whatnot that goes with that. Understood? And, a STAYCATION is even better. Find some fun things to do where you are. Stay at home and give yourself a spa treatment, soak in the tub, with Epsom salts, listen to Spa music from Pandora (they have a free app) or just give yourself a good night's rest and sleep.

3. Another way is to give yourself some beauty pampering. Go find a nice place to get a makeover. you can really boost your morale with that. The people in the salon will be happy to help. Look, you say, that's too much money. Well, but you need to spend some to be somebody. Right? So use the charge card. You have a job that pays decently, right? So if you have a balance in the card, it will get paid off in time. As long as you work. If you can't handle the job and quit that is yet another problem that you wish you didn't have.

On this subject, I must stress that looking good is a big deal in a corporate world. If you insist on wearing your hair in a silly way (like one time I saw a girl wear her hair with a knot on top of her head) and dressing like you were going to the beach, well don't expect to get any recognition even though you work your ass off all the time.

4. One other way if things are truly HOT under the COLLAR, is to find a good counselor. Somebody that will listen to you and try to figure your corporate life out. Some official societies that are specializing in your area, may offer on the job search help, or coaching. These societies are those who really care for their members and want them to succeed. That is not free, most of the time.

Or, you can find a social worker in town that will be more of a help since they would be more familiar with your town and they can suggest ways to de-stress (other than what I've suggested above). Also, some insurance companies offer what they call Employee Assistance Program, EAP, where you can confidentially

speak to someone there (who's a paid counselor) and talk about what is happening with you in your life and in your work. They are open 24/7 and they are very helpful, from what I hear.
5. One other de-stressor is playing with a loved pet. Pets are so eager to show their love. Studies have shown that petting a furry animal is able to reduce symptoms of stress.

   If pets and kids are making it so hard on you to concentrate on things at home, then you are perfectly fine with asking somebody to sit them or watch them (like a spouse or if no spouse, a pet sitter) and spend a day doing your own thing. Or, they can take the pets or kids out for a day out and then you will find time and quiet space to work on what you wish to do. It helps too when you are figuring out your checkbook, taxes, Christmas presents, and even things that the kids need to do for school projects.
6. Not to leave the significant other out of it, if you DO have one, then USE them to talk with and just chat about things that are on your mind.

When my parents were still together (she's passed on) I would hear them talk quietly about this and that, plan sometimes, or just have a quiet talk over coffee. Usually early in the morning on a weekend, I would hear them chat while I was getting up for the day. Also, schedule "date nights" where you really just spend quality time with each other without the pets or kids hanging on your knee. If you can have a date night each week, then that is great.

Some people have NO spouse or SO, which is most of the time because perhaps the career is FIRST. Well, the career is NOT FIRST. This is a big lie.

What is FIRST is that you speak to God most of all and tell Him what your plans are. God, I must stress, WILL NOT LAUGH when you speak about your plans. He made you, right? So why would He laugh at you when you tell him your earnest dreams? So, for ALL there, just know that GOD is watching and He wants to be a PART of YOUR LIFE. The career is something that will hold you body and soul together because it will pay the bills, the car and the rent/lease/mortgage. So take some time to THANK GOD that you have MOST of what you want.

Speaking of that, stress is not that toxic to people, it just means you need to take off and be by yourself or, perhaps with a SO sometime. But BE by yourself too, because you need to take care of YOU. And that means you need to ask GOD at some point in the day to see where it is you are missing something. To make it more plain, stress is NOT going to be a problem in the long run. Think of ALL those in starving nations who have nothing compared to us. Look at the gap in income between USA citizens and those in, say Laos or Nigeria. It is huge. HUGE. They may have stress there in terms of finding food and water, but they do NOT have the stress that First World people have in solving problems like the economy, etc. It might be a different stress, but would YOU trade places with them? Likely not.

I've only written a few ideas on de-stressing. One good book to read is the Harvard Business Review book on managing stress: https://hbr.org/product/hbr-guide-to-managing-stress-at-work/11960-PBK-ENG - which you can buy for a little over $20. Think about these ideas and see if putting one or more into your toolkit to heal yourself.

Image copyright:
<a href='https://www.123rf.com/profile_runzelkorn'>runzelkorn / 123RF Stock Photo</a>

The Gift of Years

• • •

It occurred to me to write about those ready for retirement. I'm at that age where retirement is looming around the corner. Yet there are times when I feel as though there are still more worlds to conquer. I heard a priest say that he too asks Jesus if this is all there is to do. If he ought to be doing something else or something more. Why we want to keep working, I ask. But this is not really work for the Man. This is work for THE Man – Jesus - God.

In my mind, there is no end to the work of God and for God. One can think of the magic age - 62, 65, or 70 that we can retire according to the government. I think that retirement is only a name. When I think of retirement, I think of an ageless Spirit that takes a person to new heights of learning. New heights of being and performing that take into account the long years that came before. It takes all the life experiences that have happened to a person distilled into focus either into one's current work or an entirely different field altogether. You may be retired at any age, but your work should always continue.

I am in the sixth decade and I find myself a graduate student again. This time I'm in creative writing. The challenge to me was whether I could reinvent myself where I will learn new things and from these, bring about good in the world.

I believe that people get thrown into the rubble of the world too soon sometimes. Fresh out of high school, I went to college and just somehow felt a bit lost. Slowly but surely I gained my moorings and became something more educated and in time, I got to be a part of a company. Yet, I think that having been through the routine career-minded ethos, I started to think and ask again: What is there more to do? Is this it? Why is it not enough?

If you feel dry in your life, and the questions are coming to you - What is left to do? What else can I do? How can I make a difference now? Then ask God to be your Guide.

It's not a matter of age at a certain point. It's a matter of that part of your mind that starts to say "Here I've accomplished much, now where can I bring this knowledge and experience?" I'd like to tell those who are thinking of looking to years of endless cruises and sitting on their easy chairs a challenge: Ask God what more you can do for Him. For those who remember JFK's words "And so, my fellow Americans: ask not what your country can do for you--ask what you can do for your country. Why don't we remember these words and make them your mantra? There are too many people who are now thinking the opposite.

A friend of mine is in her 60's and retired recently from a medical career. She now goes on medical missions to third world countries and helps heal patients. For free. She tries to get as much charity from the hospitals and other health organizations so that she can provide for those who cannot afford them.

We all aren't MDs, nor do we have that extra education to do big things. But it shouldn't stop people from opening their horizons once more. Yes, of course you have grandchildren and children. Those are first in your lives. That's a given. But there are other ways to give of you to help the world. This world is in such disquiet, a great amount of suffering, and help is not forthcoming mostly because people have turned too much inwards. If you aren't getting that nagging feeling that there ought to be more to do, then maybe you need to find it, find someone to talk to, get a little vacation somewhere where you can talk to God. Or, if you aren't sure there is a God, talk to someone who is Godly.

Age is God's gift to men and women. You must thank God for the gift of years. Thank God He gave you more time to do good, to be a part of God's family, to help the young and the very young, to find more truths to learn and impart. You can live a long and happy life if you would only ask God what more you can give. I believe wholeheartedly that with the gift of time, your sorrows and disappointments will dissolve and be made new. God is good at conversions. He will take all the boring parts, the hurting parts and the happy parts of your life and convert them into a goldmine of good things for those who need it. Be a part of something big. Think big. Think God.

Image copyright:
<a href='https://www.123rf.com/profile_mihtiander'>mihtiander / 123RF Stock Photo</a>

How to be a Team Player

• • •

THESE DAYS, COMPANIES ARE VERY eager to hire people who are or have the capability to become team players. Being in corporate for over 11 years, hiring managers I know place a great deal of respect for those in the company who are 'team players'. So what is a team player?

A team player is one who works hard not only to do well for her or himself, but to make the company goals his. It can either be by being a positive force in helping guide a project, or be somebody the team can rely on to do work. Work can be either a small piece or a larger piece of the project. Someone who, as in a marathon, can stand by to give out water to the runners or who actually stands at the different parts of the distance to help direct the runners to their right paths. A team player doesn't cherry pick what he or she wants to help with either. If the manager says you need to do something that you aren't really excited about, then you really need to step up to the plate and say "Yes, of course, I'll help". When they hear you say "I didn't get hired to do this" or "This isn't in my job description", that is actually a bad thing for you because then they remember this and when it comes time for raises or promotions, that bad thing you said is going to come back to haunt you.

People I know sometimes get the short end of a project. When I became a part of a new department, I was eager to learn and did all what was necessary to move a project along. And one project I remember was something that wasn't really a big one at all at the time. But it became one when the project reviewer asked questions that I had to answer and fast, and since my supervisor said this was my project to do as I wanted, I went and did my due diligence. Sometimes the road to becoming recognized is paved with small projects that blossom into a project people – management – will remember long after it's done. In my case, the due diligence meant that I had to reach out to outside contacts and make new contacts. So it all worked out for the best and I must say this was something I felt proud of. I still do. It isn't the sexiest project to anyone who might be watching but the project helped generate a lot of new sales that didn't get hung up because the assignment was stuck in the mud of lesser things. So, the lesson is, offer help if necessary, and be happy with the projects you have.

If you need to be pulled into a project that needed extra resources which means your really interesting project gets stuck on hold, don't be upset. This is where a team player can shine – in the sense that even if the project you get pulled into isn't (again) sexy, the company thinks it's the most important thing on their horizon. So get cracking!

Team players are good people who help the mission of an organization. Complaining, bitching, and saying that you can't do something because of some silly reason (mainly because it isn't sexy enough to work with so-and-so) won't help you stay in the company rolls. Patience is key. Do your best. See how you can make new friends in a different milieu of the company. Get crosstrained. Have fun. Don't always be the guy or girl "on the make". Being a team player is a ranking metric for a manager to base his or her judgment on who is helping instead of hindering progress.

Image copyright:
<a href='https://www.123rf.com/profile_palau83'>palau83 / 123RF Stock Photo</a>

Finessing the Transition to Manager: Advice from the Perspective of Direct Reports

• • •

HERE ARE MY SUGGESTIONS TO new managers:

If you've been working with your team as a former team mate and now are a manager (or if you come in from another company), here are a few ideas to get the buy in from your former coworkers (now direct reports) and smooth the transition:

Enjoy the bliss of the new promotion. Do all you want to do for your win – buy a new Apple watch, get a new wardrobe, spill the bucks on the new Mercedes.

Then, get back into the office and look at all the people you now manage. Be afraid. Half of these people may not work for you in the next 6 months. Don't make the following fatal mistakes:

I. Just because you are now on top of their hierarchy doesn't mean that you have the right to gloat over them
II. Or, that you can start bullying them
III. Or, that you can give them the scut work that you used to do and hated to do

Don't think that these people are now classified as "them" or "those" just because you got manager status. These people are still "us". As long as you and they work for the same company, doing the same sort of missions, and eaking out wins for the same goals – you and them are tied together.

What your job is then is to find that right attitude to manage your people. Just don't think that being promoted now makes them instantly cotton to your kind of management style.

If some of these people you now manage happen to be working and going to school at the same time, don't think that they somehow are gunning for your job.

If these employees turn in their grades to you, don't feel threatened. Let their wins be your wins.

These employees might even have more degrees than you do – don't get those degrees be in the way of your relationships. One former boss told me that he liked to hire smarter people than himself. Let their smarts make you look good and them look good at the same time. Jealousy has no place in a successful manager's toolbox.

If some of these employees are older than you, don't relegate them to the senior pile – ask them for their wise advice on everything.

Watch your talk – managers need to watch that they don't use the word "you" all the time. Use the word "we" more frequently because, as I said before, you and your employees are "we". For those managers who have problems with tact, take a class in communications. There are employees who don't like to be told they made a mistake in public, but they will appreciate that you instead sent them an email or took them aside and righted their wrongs.

Keep the employees on track not by micromanaging them but by scheduling monthly or timely meetings to keep up with their projects.

Find time to take your team out for a snack or Starbucks – they will love you for it, and, it will improve the relationships among your team mates.

When Christmas rolls along get your team mates presents to buoy their feelings of belonging to a good department and love you as their manager.

Touch base occasionally with someone who you trust in your direct reports not to give you a "yes" but that gives you the straight talk: ask them how you are doing as a manager and how does s/he think projects are getting done.

Image copyright:
<a href='https://www.123rf.com/profile_vicgmyr'>vicgmyr / 123RF Stock Photo</a>

How to Decide if You Ought to Jump Ship

• • •

IN A TYPICAL DAY, I receive emails from recruiters or emails from social media (LinkedIn, for example) where they try to tempt me and others with positions where I could be earning greater than what I currently earn. Then there are those websites that give you advice on earning more, getting raises, and so on. In terms of raises, one website states that the amount one gets as a raise is really a function of what they already earn and to get a bigger raise, one must jump to another company with a better position, etc.

For those of us who aren't that eager to move to another company (one that is in a different geographical area most of all), and who don't want the stress of uprooting family and household across the country, it is a conundrum trying to decide whether or not a raise (as prescribed above) is really worth the trouble.

In terms of whether or not to take that new job, I have a few suggestions that you might wish to consider.

First, does this job opportunity give you the best possible world to work and live in? Is there a better work/life balance? Is it worthy to have your spouse move away from what might be his/her great job where you already live? Can the children move to a school district that is better than what you already have?

Second, the one thing that seems to be a daunting aspect of moving to another job is that you never really know what you are joining. Oh, yes, there are these websites, like Glassdoor, for example, that give you the feedback and critiques of places to work. Do you really know that they have valid reasons for leaving or working there? There's a lot of personal issues people/employees are working on and that's something to consider. One also doesn't see if the work is going to be anything better than one has currently.

Third, is the work you'll be doing more challenging? If so, how much more challenging and will it, therefore, give you a chance to move up? If that is the case, are you single or married? Being single, there's a better chance to move up without leaving family abandoned one more night or weekday or weekend because you have to go on an important trip. If you're married and have children, then you need to have an understanding with your spouse that this is something that may happen. Your spouse (mainly your wife) may or may not have the necessary support system where they can look out for your family in case you are out of town for an extended period of time. Try to see if you can negotiate travel as a part of your next job opportunity.

Fourth, is the work life the same as what you already have? For some of us, better the devil we know than the devil we don't. Are you going to meet the same type of people where you're thinking of jumping to than where you are? If you don't tolerate these people where you are now, how can you in the next job? Is it worthwhile to tolerate these people given the bigger salary you'll be earning?

I would suggest that a lot of thought, meditation (prayer), and discernment needs to go through your mind before you decide to take that job elsewhere. I also suggest that you talk to everyone that you can think of (pastor, rabbi, therapist, counselor, mentor) before taking that plunge. There are a lot of people that go for that brass ring and end up hurting themselves in one way or another. For the sake of your health and peace of mind, try hard to ask these questions before making that next career leap.

Image copyright:
<a href='https://www.123rf.com/profile_alphaspirit'>alphaspirit / 123RF Stock Photo</a>

Life Lessons from the Corporate World

• • •

(PUBLISHED ON JANUARY 24, 2017 at http://womenforone.com/life-lessons-from-the-corporate-world/)

I work full time in a corporate setting. I will be working here for 11 years this year. When I first started, I was the only other person in my department besides my boss. Fast-forward to three years ago, we grew to seven people. These were made up of people raring to make their mark on the corporate world. Some were a few generations behind me. But then I realized it was time to move on. The writing had been on the wall for a while. It took me a while to understand. Corporate worlds tend to go with those who are fresh and new. I had been there too long.

Advice Number One: One cannot always be in control. Only God is in control. All. The. Time.

I think life happens when you aren't looking. Looking back, it was clear there needed to be a shift in focus, a change. It was then that I asked to move to another department where I could work on things that were more interesting to me.

Advice Number Two: In life decisions such as this, give yourself time to think it over: talk to your best advisors.

In the former place, I took a lot of stress. The job presented a great deal of challenges from different parts of the company and from outside parts, too. But I was getting burned out. It was a lot of the same old stuff, with the same old hurdles in different configurations.

Advice Number Three: Go with the flow. Let the Spirit guide you. Don't always think you have to have all the answers.

When I transferred, It felt good. I felt like the shackles of whatever imprisonment the old job had on me were freed from my hands.

Advice Number Four: What it really boils down to is whether the place you are in is where your salvation will be.

The other place I was at wasn't congruent with my salvation. Salvation in terms of better health, less stress, a new focus, a growing up.

Advice Number Five: When a job makes it challenging to behave in a Christian way, or changes you from your true self, or endangers your psychological and physical well-being, then it's time for a change.

Now that I'm in a different place, what is so great is that I have rediscovered old loves, especially writing. With my dad's help, I renovated the spare bedroom into a "studio" where I have my desk and laptop. That is where I create essays, stories, blogs, and other writing projects. I applied to grad school and now I'm in classes to obtain a master's in fine arts and creative writing.

Advice Number Six: Find where your spirit wants to grow and pursue it. Whether it is being a writer, a dancer, a poet, or a master gardener.

I feel as though what I went through two years ago was a godsend. It gave me the courage to reinvent myself. That's key to growth as a human being. Nothing is permanent. God prunes us in ways that will make us better than we were.

Life has so many possibilities, stages, and phases. We need to learn to recognize the signposts. Where to turn and how to cope. We should reach out to those who are in our lives who can see objectively, and who give good advice. We must turn to prayer and meditation. It's OK to ask God: What do you want from me? How do I cope with this dilemma?

Advice Number Seven: In looking at life, we should be courageous, bold, and creative.

Being courageous, bold, and creative was like stepping into what seemed to be an abyss. I remember someone in a retreat say: If the choice one is determining makes us feel good, then it's OK to move toward it. If it makes you feel shaky and unhappy, it's not where God wants you to go. But I realized that God was in this from the beginning. I could see His handiwork in what was happening in my life. I felt like He planted the seeds, and He gave me a thumbs-up to do the things I decided to do. He opened up my horizons, and that felt good.

There are times when I look back and feel how tough it was then. But I must shift my focus on what is here and now: homework, a new novel I'm writing, family and friends.

Advice Number Eight: Take some time to think of how things look to you at this time in your life. Pray for insight and enlightenment. There's a new world out there for everyone.

Image copyright:
<a href='https://www.123rf.com/profile_bialasiewicz'>bialasiewicz / 123RF Stock Photo</a>

The Frog in Hot Water – Is that You?

• • •

I HAVE THIS TITLE BECAUSE it's that age old story about the frog that is in a pot of water that is slowly cooking. As the story goes, the frog becomes so acclimated to the temperature that it doesn't realize until it's too late the he has been boiled dead. So my topic is about when to realize that the water temperature of your life is beginning to get too hot and it's time to get the hXX out of the pot. Don't you have these times of epiphany? Or is it so banal in your life that you just do what you do day after day and you just don't really see what's happening in your life, your career, or existence?

In terms of figuring out what is happening around yourself, I'd suggest to you that you take a mental picture of your day – or even your week. Write down on a piece of paper what it all has been like. How you felt at times during the week – and who did you talk to. If there's a lot of activity, is the activity frenetic and meaningless or is it purposeful and goal oriented?

The way out of the kettle of water can be pretty easy, if you come down to it. It's a simple thing to calmly step out of the kettle and walk away, flicking out that last drop of water from your temple.

If you think of the kettle of water as your job, for example, walking away isn't all recommended right off the bat, but what I do recommend is to see what it is that's causing the temperature to rise? Who is lighting a fire under you? Is it a boss? Is he or she the person you would rather not be working for after all? Is it a project that's taking in water? Or are people in your workplace just there voicing their complaints? Is the work too much? Do you not get any help from people in the accomplishment of projects? Are you finding it too boring?

In my experience, there are those who I worked for who were either too busy to pay attention to everyone they managed. Those bosses have gone and I have moved on. In my case, I realized that working in that field was no longer interesting. Another time where I moved on or transferred, there was just way too much noise coming from everyone around me, and it was a toxic environment.

Internally, I was feeling like there was something that wasn't being cultivated in me. The work was not enough to give me all that I thought I wanted. That was the time when I realized the job is not going to hold my hand when I needed to find guidance. Guidance had to come from some other place. I realized that there was this clamor in me wanting me to explode into a bouquet of flowers, not into a pile of body parts. The flower part of me wasn't blooming any longer. There weren't enough people around to trust, and not enough people who were in my tribe. Stepping back wasn't the way it happened for me. What happened was that I reached out of my enclosed mind and plucked at a thought – a thought that encouraged me to expand my horizons. I took an online class in writing. That was a successful class. I took another one. That went much better too. Fast forward to now, I'm halfway through my MFA in Creative Writing.

In stages, we all have that explosive event in our psyches. What you do with that is to discover what the intent is of the event. Where is it coming from? Or you could do what I did. I didn't really ask very deeply. But I felt like breaking out – exploding – and then I searched for ways to have a satisfactory answer, to get help, essentially. It also didn't hurt that I turned to prayer – a lot of it – and it helped.

So what I'm trying to say is, is that when the water where you swim is beginning to feel less than refreshing, get some time off and make a point to look backwards and then write about what it is you want to happen. You can be quite mad about your wants. Then let it sit for a day, come back to it again, and then go to work. Make a list of what you want to do to accomplish your goals – the goals that will get you into the refreshing waters of life. Don't be upset if the goals and the means to them look difficult. Breaking them into little tasks and projects will help. The one effect that this will do to your psyche is to get it to think outside the box, give it a sense of relief – that help is coming. That you're noticing your own life and its current state.

Image copyright:
<a href='https://www.123rf.com/profile_theblackrhino'>theblackrhino / 123RF Stock Photo</a>

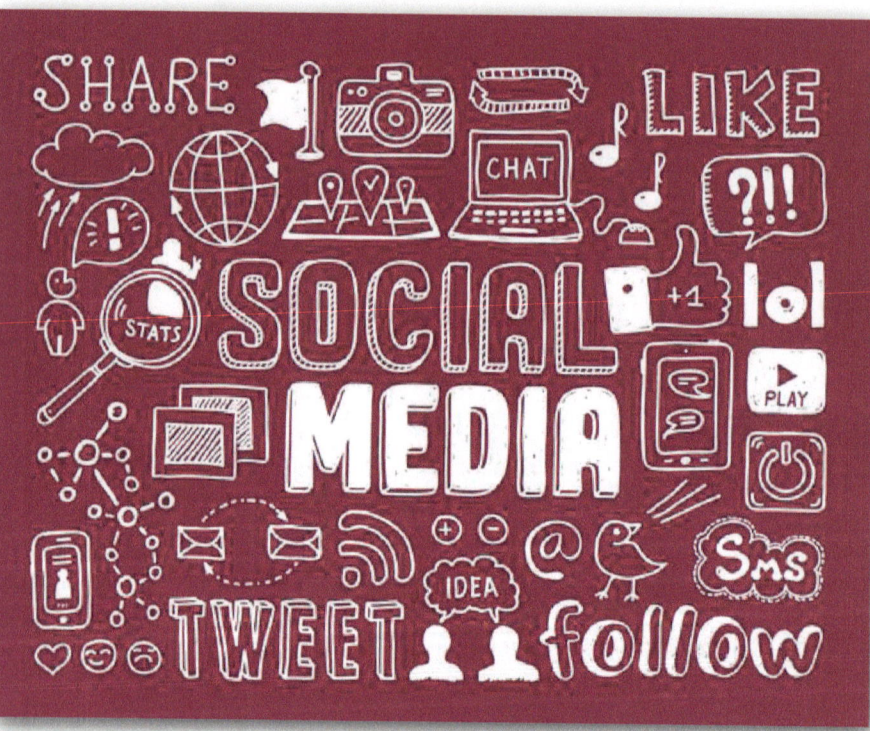

What are Some of the Advantages and Disadvantages of Using Social Media to Get a Job After College?

• • •

SOCIAL MEDIA IS SO INGRAINED in the culture of today. The advent and eventual boom of the smartphone has replaced the need to find up to date news and socially relevant events in the print media. Facebook is almost in every smartphone, and other social media apps including LinkedIn, Twitter, Instagram, to name a few are sitting cheek by jowl next to each other in cell phones and in browsers of users, eager to find out the newest in every aspect of society. The businesses that wish to be current and in the conversations of Facebook users, or in the culture of the world find that they must always also use and spread their messages and mission values on social media.

In the world of students, social media allows for greater reach of students to look into the world of businesses from where they sit. It is so easy for somebody to see what others are doing. Where they eat, sleep, have vacations, and work. It is so easy for a college graduate to find out what businesses are tweeting, blogging or FBing. The kind of work people do is always on display – from employers who want others to see the type of culture their business has, to actual employees who FB blog about the kind of events their employer hold. It is almost like breathing – one can always filter out social media from their consciousness, but it is almost as accessible as reaching for something to write with.

When using social media to find employment, there are advantages as well as disadvantages. In terms of advantages, a smart college graduate can see into the employers' social media to know if their business, their products or their mission values are what the new graduate wishes to incorporate in their lives as employees. The graduate can find out as well whether that business is searching for new employees. It is not hard to go on LinkedIn and see what jobs are out there – who is working for that company and whether one can send them a connecting invite or an InMail. For a few more dollars a month, the searching graduate of a college can even look at the statistics that a business may have accumulated in terms of the number of employees hired in the year, how much money that business is willing to pay for someone who successfully achieves that job that has been posted, and how many people work for them. In social media, the searching college graduate can look at the types of people who work for a business – in the tweets they make about working there, in the schools and profiles they have on their LinkedIn page and in their resumes which is available for viewing. There are even tips on social media to find a job and how to find employment in a certain company. The tips include: connecting with these employees, looking at their profiles and matching them with the goals the job seeker may have for their own careers. There are also those who use social media to connect with friends and directly ask them what their experiences are working where they are. Or what they think of living in the area where that company has a presence.

In social media such as LinkedIn, it is also possible to find out how many people have applied for a job, what their qualifications are, and whether the applicant's qualifications measure up to the job's qualifications are. It is also possible to see how much that position may pay in salary as compared to others.

Twitter is a great way to see what employees of a company tweet about their employers. The number of followers of a company on Twitter may attest to the popularity of their company. The actual tweets that a company posts may be a gold mine to a graduate applicant in terms of how much culture the company has, how relevant their products and services are, and how much education their employees may have. Tweets can also be ways to understand what the company's issues may be and whether the job applicant can handle them, or even give the applicant a way to talk to the hiring managers about how s/he can help the company out with a sticky problem that s/he saw in their Twitter page.

One can also find out through social media about what the company likes – who they like, what other businesses they like, or work with. It is also easy to find out the type of environment the company is located in – is there a compatibility with the work/life balance or the actual environment the applicant desires to live in.

In terms of work/life balance, one can find out about a company's philosophy by looking at social media. The graduate applicant can perform a search on Facebook about different aspects of work and life balance. There are also other sources to find out about work/life balance of a company. One example is in LinkedIn – connecting with recruiters on LinkedIn is a common way to find jobs. For those starting out after school, recruiters are somewhat reluctant to represent them due to the lack of experience. However, a job applicant can reach out to recruiters and even current employees of a company to ask about work life balance. It may be better to reach out to recruiters because they are more detached and have a standard which they base their opinions on.

When interviewing a new applicant, employers usually ask him or her what it is about their company that attracted them. An applicant can easily respond by saying that the company's social media page was an impetus for them to apply. Applicants have a great tool in social media to provide intelligent answers to the interview questions.

Social media also provides a way, not too often, to see the type of clothes the employees of a company wear in a given day. This is mostly a company culture aspect which the job seeker can gauge against his or her own philosophy of what suits their sense of style. Is the company something that requires only business apparel, or are they more casual? One can also see on social media the types of employees that the business hires: are they young or mature? Does it matter to the job seeker? Can the job seeker find compatibility in the profiles of the people who work for that company?

How long a company has been in business can be found in social media, as well as in company website pages. If the business is a startup or an established company, social media can give clues to it. If the business has an international presence, that can be seen on social media.

It doesn't cost anything to like a company's page on Facebook. It is also free for anyone to create a LinkedIn page. The popularity of these sites is what drives companies to having a social media presence. Job seekers like college graduates that are comfortable navigating social media should always look up a company they wish to work for on social media.

There are disadvantages to the use of social media for college graduates in seeking jobs. One of them is that there is an unreliability to some forms of social media in that only the positive aspects of working in a company are displayed. No business wants their problems in hiring or ethics displayed in their social media pages. Businesses are loath to talk about their dirty laundry, much more on social media. What is not seen may be more important than what is seen. It is important for the job seeker graduate to understand that businesses have to be rated in terms of their mission, their effectiveness, the successes of their products and their failures. These metrics also include things like their profit for the year, how they performed in the market, what the forecast is for their business. It is also important to know whether they have a social conscience – are they involved in community outreach? Are the company officers ethical and aboveboard in their relationships with their customers? Twitter is a good way to see whether unsatisfied customers are tweeting about how badly some business had treated them. It is almost guaranteed that when someone tweets about a bad customer experience, that business will immediately tweet back that they are willing to help that customer find satisfaction.

Another disadvantage to using social media is that the actual salary of the position advertised is not accurately cited and it may actually never be known until the time the applicant is asked to sign on the employment contract. There are other sources of finding out about compensation, and these are not in social media per se. It is something that graduates need to understand and factor in when searching for a job. Sometimes, salaries posted next to the job advertised do not factor in the educational attainments of the employees that do get that salary. At most times, the salary posted is a ballpark figure, and it is not helpful in gaining interest in the job – something that is mostly to the detriment of the applicant who may turn away from applying when s/he sees that the salary is lower than what they desire.

Social media cannot always tell the truth about what it is to work for a company. Sometimes the company would rather not have a social media page due to fears of being sued by not giving a fair and balanced advertisement of their products. For example, there are medical device or pharmaceutical companies who are bound by law to provide a pro and con on the use of their products when advertising on social media or any print or electronic website. If an applicant were to understand well how the company's future presence will be in the world of business, it is necessary to find out whether the company manufactures good and sound products. Their sound business presence and profile will assure the job seeker graduate that if they land a job in that company, they will likely keep their jobs and even be promoted if they work hard enough.

Social media cannot be relied upon to give a fair opinion or review of businesses (see above). When social media is worst is that bias can come from those who operate that social media page – the founders of Facebook or Twitter or Instagram. There are reports that say that Facebook has been accused to promoting some businesses or personalities over others, sometimes in subtle ways. Advertisement from companies can skew the stories that social media tell about them.

Social media can also make it look like a company is the best place to work in – instead of focusing on the real bits and pieces that make a company good and reliable; one is given soft portrayals of emotional advertisement that is generated from the company's marketing department. The bits and pieces that make a company a reliable one – that is, a company that can promise a good salary and compensation – come in different forms and may lie outside the bounds of what a social media can provide. These bits and pieces can take the form of product reviews, new blockbuster products that are in the pipeline (but not yet available in advertisements) and employee turnover rates. It would be incumbent upon a job seeker out of college to do their due diligence in order to find a good starting position at a good company.

As a result, the successful job applicant may still be at a disadvantage in that once s/he gets the job that job may not be as s/he had initially thought it to be. It is easy to take a job from a company which doesn't have much on their social media page and cleverly puts together a glib advertisement about a job opening.

Social media doesn't have or employ reliable reviews of companies either. One sees many five star reviews on a company's Facebook page but are any of these reviews truthful or accurate? The number of disgruntled ex-employees could pepper the pages with one star comments. Alternately, competitors of that company could give the page multiple black marks (one star reviews). The college graduate has to be almost prescient to look past the reviews and understand that truth doesn't reside in social media pages and their reviews.

Image copyright: <a href='https://www.123rf.com/profile_bloomua'>bloomua / 123RF Stock Photo</a>

Independence

• • •

I'VE STARTED MY OWN COMPANY and it's been up for over a year now. It's my company on writing - based on advice from an accountant at Writers Digest - and now I am the sole owner of an LLC business. I recently left my full time job and that has become a bit of a challenge in a good way. I am now challenged daily to have a work schedule that will focus ONLY on my work, my business, and making it grow. I have a fund to work with - savings, really - and I have signed up with a shared office space within which to do the mundane things of putting up my laptop and writing in relative peace. I can't always write at home, especially with cats jumping on my desk and wanting a pet, or with my dog snoozing at my feet and getting all antsy once I am astir, to beg for treats at each moment that I'm not stuck at my home desk.

I don't really miss the work meme - that sort of atmosphere of being amongst people in a company - not yet, anyway. A friend of mine who worked for a company as a remote employee told me that she missed her cube mates. But I'm not that sort of person even at work where I liked to chat with cube mates and meet at the kitchen to pour out coffee and comment on the day's activities. In my more mature years, that loner label has been cast at my direction more than once. I accept that, and yet to some, the loner label is anathema. Why is that? I don't know. I like the idea of going at things alone, yet there is always that Higher Power that moves me and so I really am not alone. Perhaps, in the work mode, team playing is big and that is what people are comfortable with. Being a loner at a corporate level is not good, if I read these corporate types right. I can see why, they all need your input, they need your gut feelings on decisions and so on. I seem to digress but perhaps this is part of the reason why I am going on my own. I don't want to have to work for somebody on projects that no longer appeal.

My work then is my writing. The stuff that my dreams are based on. I can be sure that if I spend time struggling with a document's formatting (which I did yesterday with rather desperate results!), I can say that I am working on my stuff so I don't consider it a waste of 'company' time. I find it hard to think of some (digressing here) documents that are templates really, and make them into what I want them to be. I think that the time to self-teach (go to and take some short courses on say, Microsoft Word?, lol) is here. But, I would rather spend all my time learning how to create document templates (stationery, e.g.) than having to create hyperlinks to documents that go to an internal database that would never really be helpful to anyone but the person working on the document. This sort of thing actually happened at my former workplace. Imagine hyperlinking almost every word or term in documents for a stretch of days at a time? No it was time to quit. LOL.

I am grateful for the independence from a job that has become onerous. I may one day work part time to supplement my business, but that might not ever come because, hey, maybe God will send me a publishing contract (smile). However, it may be in my future, I think I'll be ok. I think that despite the risks involved in putting up my shingle at my age, I think I will be ok. I give all to My God, and to His direction. That is what keeps me from going into a stark reality that seems to cloud minds and reduce the creativity in this world.

I would suggest those who wish to strike out on their own to do it soon, but to find their passion first. And, more importantly, to ASK GOD for Guidance and Patience. Things will one day be ok. But the good part is that getting there will be filled with many moments of fun and good feelings. Imagine yourself in your own place, in your own office, having a cup of tea or coffee, wandering into the kitchen and finding snacks, petting the dog, and then going back to work. I think that's an ideal life. And an ideal workplace.

Image copyright:
<a href='https://www.123rf.com/profile_sunshinesmile'>sunshinesmile / 123RF Stock Photo</a>

Happiness

• • •

Is a state of mind, right? So, today I am happy that many of the viewers have looked at the post about Title of Work. I hope everyone feels free to comment. I won't ask for names, of course. Just give us a nudge and tell us that this resonates. Or maybe it might be awakening some thought in your mind to see whether this sort of intention is there somewhere. Remember that God reads our souls, our minds. Just a FYI. I don't mean to proselytize, but in writing fiction, don't we all say something anyway? Remember Walker Percy and his Moviegoer novel? I learned there that we are all somehow bystanders that give some support to others as they pass through our lives. As writers of fiction, we have an obligation to make a statement of what our work is about. We just can't keep writing stuff that's going to boggle minds because they are filled with unrelated abusive stuff, and hope that the novels are held together somehow by sheer suspension of disbelief. No, we all must stand for something. We all must say what's in our hearts, what's in our minds and what moves us to write. The characters in LR have been friends now to me, they speak to me about what they like to say, how they want to say it and even what they like to wear. It's something I've learned in MFA classes. Characters are alive in your mind, then in your story and then they live on in the minds of those who read them. If they are lucky, they become alive in movies that are made from the novels. But it is always a way to introduce memorable people. I like to be kind to my characters. I want them to grow up, or change for the better. Those characters that have flaws, they may have to be rehabilitated, or at worst, they need to go to prison or be somehow in some way made to take stock of what they have done and be attentive to it, how they've gotten that way, and well, that's what prisons do, don't they?

I hope that in some way, my fiction will touch people and make someone make a phone call, or write a letter, or email someone or even just reach for a memory of when things were good in their lives. It isn't too late, no, not at all. At this stage of my life, it wasn't too late to make a leap of faith to become writer. It is NEVER too late. Not to me, anyway. Please God that is not too late for anyone else who really wants to change.

Image copyright: <a href='https://www.123rf.com/profile_jakkapan'>jakkapan / 123RF Stock Photo</a>

Last Things

• • •

The final goodbye
The way West
The only road
The questing eye
The one who got away
The rose on the vine
The happy embrace
The wayward fool
The ticket to London
Every exit open
Total excess
Life that matters
Elohim thoughts
Guidance of angels
Altars of gold
Heaven's gate
Love everlasting
The One the True
God alone

Image source: www.commons.wikimedia.org

My Rant on the Closing of Our Marsh Store

• • •

I AM DEALING WITH PROGRESS in my little town. We have had a large influx of new settlers here, some from different parts of the world, some from neighboring towns, some just temporarily – students, I mean. And with these new settlers the large companies have decided to set up their own flagship buildings. Some companies, though, have left. And one of them, our Marsh store in West Lafayette, has decided to close. There are other bigger box groceries in town. So, I suppose that was what drove our little Marsh store off the grid. We have Meijer, Walmart, Kroger-Payless, and even some smaller groceries that serve the university studentship. We won't mention them, in case the business gods want them to leave as well.

Our little Marsh store was not a little one at all. It had all the amenities: the deli, the bakery, the flower shop, and, it had international items (like Chinese and English fare). It had a navigable footprint, we knew where to find things – and it wasn't a long slog like with Walmart where you could easily get lost in it looking for vitamins or Coffee or canned meat.

When my family settled here in the early 90's, the Marsh store was pretty much the only store in town, perhaps the Kroger one was also up. But Kroger had a large store and it was difficult to park in it. I had visions of being t-boned in their parking because someone didn't look behind to see who was driving past. So Kroger, despite being a serviceable store, seemed a bit of a risk to me.

Marsh had friendly people, the greengrocers liked to say hello and helped when I couldn't find the pine nuts for my recipe. The manager, who I just met a few months ago (he'd been there for years) had informed me then that they weren't going out of business, they really are doing a profit and so the fear of them closing had dissipated. But that was then, the news, the cold hard news is that they are now being run off the grid of West Lafayette.

It is a difficult thing to see something that's been there for decades and been the provider of your food and greens and alcohol since you started and made this place your own. My own, as it were. I know that another bigger, fancier store will come out and replace it. It will tear down the building and who knows what other ones attached, and it will be a mess for a while and then it will announce itself.

Maybe that is progress. But what progress really, for the manager who told me he was glad they weren't closing because he is a couple of years away from retirement? Or the green grocers who have aged through the years, and still look as young as they were with just a bit of grey around the gills – where do they go? I know that they will be taken care of, at least, that is what I hope Marsh will do – give them a good retirement package. But the memories will go away.

Memories of Marsh you say? Well, we had friends who were the cashier, the ones who sold us our lotto tickets, the assistant manager who offered to keep an eye on my dog while I shopped, the friends we bumped into and regaled with news of our latest trips or retirements and so on. Where will they be next? I doubt that there will be a greater chance to see them again – where would they be? What do people do when their favorite store closes? Are the alternatives going to be ok? What will I miss most about Marsh?

I guess I will miss a few things about Marsh, besides what I have already said. I will miss their ample parking (mostly due to the fact that hardly anyone shopped there anymore) where I could actually sit and scroll through my newsfeed on Twitter in my parked car, or, where I would eat my Starbucks Danish before going in to shop. I will miss its accessibility. I will miss well, the past. I guess that is what I will miss. The past that includes my whole family shopping there and now the family has dwindled. So, perhaps that is what I will miss about Marsh. Those scenes in the past where Marsh figured in some way. Not greatly, but in a significant way.

Small towns are the thing of the past, though. Our town is eager to be part of the next technological super age. So, with that, let all small grocery stores beware. One can't always stay the same, one must do what they can to matter to those who are around. Those who have patronized Marsh are in their later years, those who are more inclined to want to shop safely, to feel like there's a warm place to go and feel like they belong. The youth of the town will go where they have access to Starbucks, to new-fangled foods, to every type of monster drink available. The rich will always go where the parking lot is paved and has no bad holes. The entrepreneurs will go where there are party stuff to celebrate openings and launches. And then where would these stores be that can't have all for these demographical shoppers?

Perhaps that is what Marsh needed – and they tried to keep up, they tried to stock those things that only they would carry and not others. They installed U-scan devices, and made the store more spacious. But, too little too late.

I fear for those who will miss Marsh that they will completely be in a catatonic state when they enter a big box store. What of those tender hearts who really only wanted one item and then scurry back home to cherish it with their recipe?

I might be getting too maudlin, but I really really hate that Marsh is closing here. I know I'll get over it. I shouldn't fret, of course, because perhaps it is part of God's plan. Yes, He has a plan even for Marsh stores. I don't know what that would be, but in God's Mind, these things are present. So for all Marsh aficionados, take heart. God's in control. He will be happy to hear our fears and settle them in his Fatherly way.

The Dream

• • •

VERY OFTEN I HEAR OR read of people who express their dreams for their lives. Many dreams are common among people: success, a house that's in a great neighborhood, a car – maybe one that's new and has a status emblem on the hood. Other dreams are also about success for their children, or loved ones, or dreams of good health or beating the Big C. There are dreams to travel abroad and get to know other cultures. There are dreams that are immediate. Like dreams to pay off debt, win the lottery, have one's own business, make it big, marry the best person.

Many dreams are built on good foundations. The foundations might include: a good education, a job that's steady, a life free of addictive behaviors, being part of a faith community. These foundations most definitely are good stepping stones to achieving dreams. Yet there are dreams that seem almost impossible because the foundations are not sound.

Take for example the dream to become a citizen of a country. This dream is great especially for people who want to find good places to raise their children. To give their children a good chance at life. Better lives than where they were born. I think this is the dream that's a hard one for people these days to achieve. At this time in the US, the things that keep dreamers out of this goal include crime, poverty, addiction and the wrong friends. These foundations, if you can call them foundations, aren't good to base dreams on.

While these 'foundations' are like the shifting sands in the Gospel that speaks of building a house on solid rock, one shouldn't feel dismayed that one can never achieve their dreams. I don't propose to give solutions to those whose dreams are built on shifting sands because everyone's case is different. But I do propose to encourage all dreamers to pray for their dreams to come true.

Dreams take time to come true. It's not at the end of 'get rich quick' schemes. Like paying off enormous debt, the monthly submission of payments can be all one need to do, plus avoiding the pitfalls of falling off the plan like spending again on credit.

There's a lot to be said about patience as well. One of the virtues, patience can be the lifeline to a person who dreams. Who even dream big. If one waits long enough, that dream goal may be attainable because of an unexpected blessing.

God never said not to dream big dreams. He is, after all, the Source of ALL riches, the Source of Eternal Life. We are His children, aren't we? Didn't He say: "Knock and you shall enter, Ask and you shall receive, Seek and you shall find?" Those who count themselves as God's children can count on asking God for their needs, and yes, even the big dreams. It's a great way to start the conversation. That conversation is called Prayer. To pray, one can begin with a short invocation with any of the following: Come Holy Spirit. Come and help me, God. I place myself in Your Presence, O Lord. Be with me, Lord.

One will find that as prayer deepens, God works in our lives and sees where you need to make changes. He intervenes and places opportunities in your path. He removes obstacles to your goals. In many cases, it's what might be called a process of conversion. You might find that your dreams change because God gives you a better way of looking at things. And then the dreams are more meaningful when they come true. They are more meaningful to you because God made these just for you and your circumstances.

Image copyright:
<a href='https://www.123rf.com/profile_evgenyatamanenko'>evgenyatamanenko / 123RF Stock Photo</a> - the dream

Image source: maxpixel.freegreatpicture.com

The Learning

• • •

FROM THE MOMENT OF INFANCY, children are taught to learn about things – eating to survive, crying to get attention, smiling to get more love and attention. Then as toddlers children learn to crawl, then walk, and this is all a process that has gone on from the beginning of all time. God was there always, giving the child the means to find a way to survive and iive and thrive. When children go to school, there is the learning to make the mind facile and inquisitive. To watch their teachers and learn what they are taught, to take on the attitudes of their friends and elders. They sit at home at the kitchen table or dinner table and listen to their parents and grandparents talk of politics, and manners and people who have been significant in their lives. If the children are lucky, there are books to read and devour and learn from to think more, to have the ideas with which to reach for intangible things – life, love, happiness and that one thing that they will always strive for – Heaven.

Yet something gets in the way, doesn't it? Have you seen it happen too many times? Our young children start to follow the wrong things and people. They ape their heroes and heroines - they smoke, take drugs, dress like harpies, get into bed too soon with the wrong ones, and then they bring all these hurts and take them to new relationships and jobs and cities and all of that follows. Their parents, we – or their elders - the aunts and uncles – we sit helpless. We remember how these children are and were, when they were just from the womb, wrapped in blankets and bonnets. All slightly wrinkled and toothless. Smiling up at someone, not us, but at some other One who looked down at them and gave them that spark of life.

So what happens with the learning? Where did the learning go wrong? Who made this learning fall into a pit of snakes? I do think that smoking is the first thing that happens to a child – it happened to me. I went to work at a hospital in my first job while in collge. In that hospital, I was with a group of ICU nurses and staff. They all would gather in one of the empty rooms and have a smoke. I was there and felt out of place. So I smoked too. My Dad found out – my room reeked of smoke and the ashtray was under my bed. He was a calm and authoritative man, and told me to stop smoking. There was something in his voice that told me that he meant business. And so I did stop smoking.

But what of the others who pass through without an authority figure in their lives, smoking cigarettes then on to weed, then cocaine and then on to oblivion?

These are the ones that you might call "lucky" because their lives are short but miserable. They don't wreak havoc on their loved ones, they miss out on the people who would have helped them back on track, they don't get into more trouble, cause fires, cause heartbreak, or God knows what else. They learn the wrong things. They reach for the people who tell them this is the Good Life. They like the fast cars, the big mansions, the easy money, the fashionable houses - the modeling, the grimy cities that promise success.

The Learning I am talking about is the Learning that tells a child that this is the true way and the path to getting OLD. Yes, OLD. Why do the young live a short life and then die into oblivion? Because they made a choice to learn and reach for things that led them to death. You can do that math – that connection of dots. Think on your own lives and the lives of those who never made it past 18 or 25 or 30.

Why did I want to talk about Learning today? Because we all keep learning Something. What that Something is, is really a cooperation between you and God. Yes, God. Here's that God word again, you say. Well, it's true. Here's another word – Satan. A child is a big deal to both God and Satan. Satan wants the children. He is salivating even now to snatch a child into his clutches and make this child become him and be as evil as sin and as death. There are so many of these seemingly untouched children out there. They made the wrong choices and reached for the bad things in the world. And then they use the knowledge that only Satan can give them and make others sad, suffer, or die. Every day.

The Learning is an important concept. God taught us that first Learning. In Eden. Each of us goes through The Learning in our own Eden. Who is the serpent in your life? What will you and your children do when the serpent lifts its rattle and tells you to eat that luscious 'apple'? Where will you find recourse? Who will you call to get you out of the pit of vipers? What will you say or pray? Will there be grace to give you to pray and call God's name? If you do call God's name, then the Learning will have been successful because God hears you when you utter His name. And He will take you back into His loving arms to heal and forgive.

The Lesson I Learned

• • •

WRITERS DON'T CARE HOW THEY look. What is important to them is what they write about. You can look like a wreck and write the most beautiful prose. You can have wart on your nose and write a lovely poem. Writers have no wish to attain the heights of beauty. Not in the physical sense. Their world is in words, in worlds, in heaven or in some part of hell where a little bit of life still thrives.

I went to a writer's conference last year. The keynote speaker was a woman who was a writer in residence at a university. She looked like someone's old maid aunt. She wore no makeup, her hair was disheveled from the wind, her clothes weren't designer clothes. They were the clothes of a journeywoman. Someone who just came out of a long trip on the road.

Yet when she read her work I began to hear and see her world, Her humor and her wit. Yes, she was a writer. Not a thing about her physically that would cause a lot of heads to turn. But turn they did when they heard her speak.

So I learned a lesson that day. I felt like I could be comfortable as a writer. I didn't need makeup. I didn't need a lot of hair product nor did I need to wear the latest fashions to be with other writers. Or, to write on my laptop. In class, my classmates and I, get along well discussing what I loved doing: Writing. What we did was enough. And that was to write, and write well.

And part of the lesson for me was to look at others without judging them based on their appearance. It is not how God wants us to treat people. We need to look into their eyes, their smiles, the creases on their brows, the rough edges of their lives and come to understand how God made them the way they are and see how they work, what they do.

Each of us has a purpose in life. Don't let the way we look to each other get in the way.

The Lie

• • •

I AM GOING TO GO out on a limb and say that the Evil Satan is the Leader of this world. He is the Father of Lies. Lie No. 1 - You have to be rich to be happy. Lie No. 2 - You have to move up in the world to be successful and happy. Lie No. 3 - You need to be pretty and smart to be happy and successful. Lie No. 4 - The world is the only place that matters. Lie No. 5 - The happiness you seek is in drugs, food and sex.

I am sure that I will be pilloried by those who follow these lies and believe in them. That is not going to stop me at all. There are millions of people in the world who are happy without these things - the trappings of success. Lies are so rampant that people make concrete structures from them. A building can be a tissue of lies, wrapped with words, documents, products, and profit margins. It is a lie to think that a company is successful because it has a good profit.

Do you believe everything that is seen by the stock market? Is the stock market a lie in itself? Why do people invest in it? It is a lie too.

We are all sitting on unsteady ground. None of us are really secure. The Father of Lies webs us all up in his magic and makes us believe he is real and will give you all you need. This is what WE are up against. Those who manufacture lies and follow the Evil One are destined to be like the weeds that are burned after a harvest.

Those who feel that they are given a God-given talent and want to pursue success must listen avidly to God's prodding and making them depend upon His Divine Providence. This is what God wants from the world. It is not enough to feel that God is present when you go to daily Communion. It is more important to feel that God is listening to you and you ask Him for guidance. It is always good to question the thoughts that come to you and make you want something or someone. Always ask God what to do. He will answer.

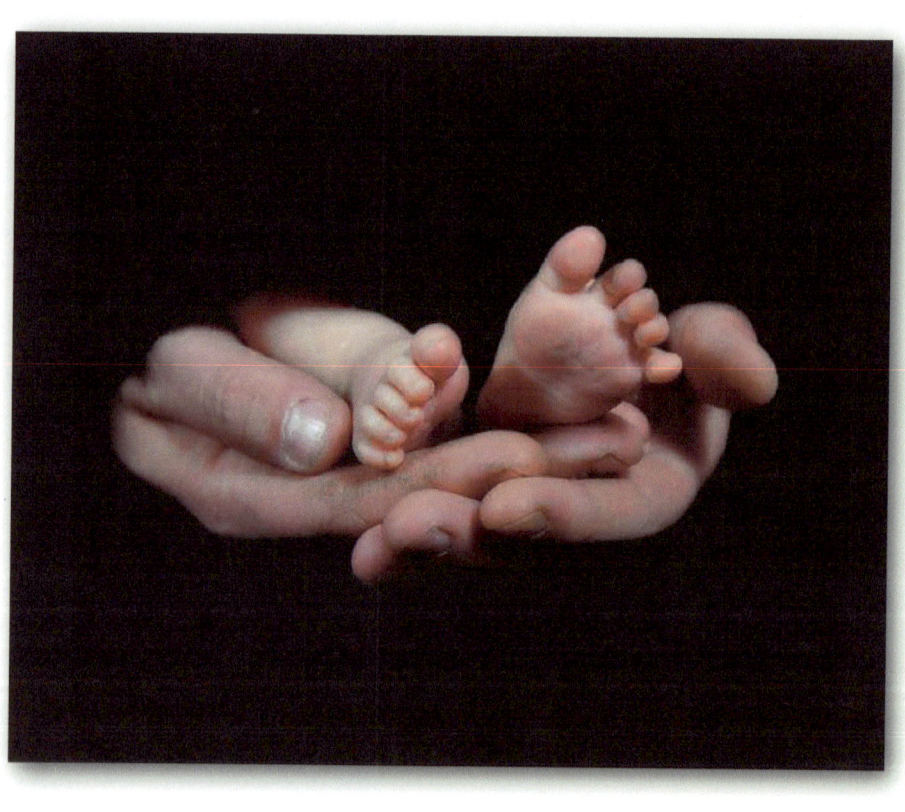

The Nurturing

• • •

WHAT ABOUT NURTURE?

Coming to my mind - in Oxford University (UK), they have a practice or tradition of students being in meetings with their professors - a one to one kind of meeting to discuss and improve their work, and to write essays and papers. This appealed to me because I believed this was the right way to become educated. I love the idea of Oxford and being a student there.

In my life, nurturing is a big deal - my parents nurtured me, mostly my Mom who was my guide and mentor in all things. My father stood as the disciplinarian, the one who told me once to quit smoking and was the Voice of Authority.

As an only child, I wanted and sought out nurturers in my life. There were few. Besides my Mom, these may have been friends and teachers and in my graduate life, that was my PhD major professor. He wasn't too nurturing as he was busy. But, he made sure that I was 'protected' from those who would wish to tear my project apart. He came to all my presentations, and then asked me what my wish would be - do I want to become an MD or a PhD? Or did I want to major in Biochem or in Pharmacology. These are not at all out of the ordinary for a major professor to do, but that was something I appreciated. And it was nurturing. And, he enjoyed eating the Asian food I brought to work when we celebrated birthdays and achievements.

Nurturing children to become good students is a key thing. Nurturing students to succeed in their chosen field of study is most important. The trajectory of nurturing is in direct opposition to the progress of an individual's growth, I fear. I fear that there are no older guides who are there to see to it that a growing or young adult is on the right path to becoming the best they can be. In terms of work, the ones who appear to be nurturers besides the management and higher levels of the company would be the human resources director and her staff. I know from experience that she would be checking to make sure everything was where and how they ought to be. That they are happy, content, filled with new projects etc.

But it isn't really enough, though is it? To my mind, nurturing is mainly relegated to babies and nurseries. When the babies have been let out of school in the 7th grade, they are almost done with nurturing them. In church, nurturing is good as well, and this activity can be in the care of children while the parents are being given religious 'food' but the best part is when the children go to Sunday School. The nurturing there happens only on Sundays, and then the rest of the child's life is taken to the four winds the rest of the week.

What I'm trying to say in so many words, though, is that we ALL NEED CONSTANT NURTURING. Self-love, maybe so - and that is the topic of another blog post (see MarianMusings.com). But, I mean - that love of a better and older, wiser person - those would be our parents. It behooves us Parents to nurture our children NO MATTER how old they are. To those who have no parents remaining, there are the aunts and great aunts, the grandparents and godparents. In the tradition of baptism, the godparents are given the task of taking over the raising of children of the family if both parents were to die suddenly before the children are of adult age.

Seek out the nurturers in your world. If you see the sign at the office "Your Mother DOES NOT WORK HERE" that only means you need to bus your tables and clean up after you have had your morning coffee. But it seems to hint at the fact that one cannot expect a "mother" or "nurturer" in that office.

It seems to me that the workplace is where nurturers are lacking. I don't see supervisors being nurturers where I have worked. It seems that all work is geared towards the production of something. Not of someone. I suppose you can't really expect a company to turn out better employees. Yet, isn't that something that one could expect? Why not? If one were to go to another company and tell them they worked for A and company B is thinking "I've seen A employees and boy, they are great!" Is not that a good sign that A company was somehow nurturing? I don't mean diaper changes and timely readings of bedtime stories. NO, I mean, that the company needs to improve the education of their employees in a nurturing way.

If a company fails an employee, that is deserves thirty lashes of a leather splint across the back. Well, I'm being facetious. But if an employee is someone who has had many good things to say and many good projects that they've done, and that company has marginalized that employee without much ado, then I'd say the company is comatose and is on life support.

Of course, nurturing an employee can be dangerous, can't it? There are those who don't think their coworkers should be nurtured. Why that person and not me? Then if that happens, nurturing must be equitable. But there are elements of fairness that aren't present in many companies. It is then that an employee needs to decide whether he or she is in need of nurturing elsewhere. Or, if one can't move or is somehow beholden to that company, then the nurturing must definitely come from "extraterrestrial" sources.

I'm finding that this is how everyone must seek their Nurturers. I am suggesting that one seek Sunday school all over again. Sundays for nurturing the individual is perfect. One goes to have church services, and then maybe a hearty lunch, and then a little nap and then settle down to read, or write about how things could be improved in one's life. Taking the ideas of what was discussed at church service and putting those against what one is going through in life. I'm suggesting a prescription of nurturing - asking a Higher Being to be part of one's life and becoming THE ONLY and ONE NURTURER. It's simple enough. Father God, you would begin, help me here because I need nurturing.

Image copyright:
<a href='https://www.123rf.com/profile_donnaallard'>donnaallard / 123RF Stock Photo</a>

The Object in My Junk Drawer

• • •

THERE IS AN OBJECT IN my junk drawer. It is my New York City Public Library Card. I don't really think it is a junk piece. Not at all. I used to live in New York (Queens), back in the late '80's. There was a branch of the library a block from my workplace. That was on 1st Avenue and 68th street. Or was it 67th? I would go to the library to borrow books and actually lug them home (walk to the subway, in the subway waiting for the train to arrive, at subway stop where I lived, on the walk home). I don't know how I managed to bring books home all the way from Manhattan.

I totally love libraries, and the NY Public Library is such a big and great place to find books of all kinds. The card is laminated, has a lion on the front, just like the lion statues on the front of the main library and the text that shows my name is in a maroon color.

I found, while I lived in NY, that New Yorkers loved to read on the subway, in the park, in any place where there was a chair and a coffee to drink. In the subway, one didn't just stare into space. They read books, mostly to relieve the boredom of the train ride, and to avoid eye contact.

I don't know now how New Yorkers read their books. Do they have their Kindle? Or read on their iPhone Kindle app? Or do they actually hold an honest-to-God paperback or hardback? I would guess technology would trump tradition in this case. It is easier to read with a Kindle or iPhone, jostled by other subway riders or hanging by the straps trying not to fall into someone's space.

I am proud to hold a library card from NYC PL. It is something so authentically New York. I should put the card in a frame and have it on display at my desk. Like a badge of having been through life in New York city.

This library card is a symbol of my literary journey. I will keep it safe to remind me that the journey is just getting into a groove.

This library card is also a symbol of hope – hope that one day at least one book of mine will share the shelves of the books in the NYCPL or at least, in our own city library. I don't really know, however, whether a book, once published, would automatically get added to the NYCPL catalogue of books. In my city library, the members of the library have to submit book suggestions for their library to buy. Not all of their suggestions are taken up. I find that daunting. I now look at my library card and try to remember what books I actually checked out of the NYCPL. Most likely, bestsellers. In fiction, in romance, or mystery. What else would someone who once worked for a living by growing human cells do to relax their mind?

Image copyright: <a href='https://www.123rf.com/profile_tommroch'>tommroch / 123RF Stock Photo</a>

The Separator

• • •

I sat in church one Sunday and listened to a homily by a young priest who explained how the Devil gets his victims and kills their souls. In essence, what the devil does is this: He separates us from our loved ones, from those who really and truly care for our welfare and would do ANYTHING to make us happy. How does he do this? Well, I can think of a lot of ways the devil does it. But let's go back to that homily. That one essential thing that the Devil makes people die (spiritually and then eventually, finally separating our souls from God) had come at a time in my life where I was in a lot of stress at work.

There was someone in my workplace, someone who seemed like a friendly sort and she was a new person there. We had some things in common, and she was about a few years older than me. She had been through a few job changes in her life. She was hoping that this job would be the last before she retired. We had several times when we shared a lunch or just had a short chat at work at our desks. Then I became aware that she was slowly trying to make me do things her way. Look at things her way, and even to the point where she was criticizing my religion, my faith.

One time, it was after I went to Ash Wednesday services at my church and I was sporting a huge ashen cross on my forehead, she met me for lunch and then she laughed at me. She said that this Ash thing was "not serious" and "not necessary". I protested that Yes it WAS serious for me.

Then, she mentioned in passing that her neighbor had the statue of the Blessed Virgin Mary in his back yard and it was in full view of my coworker when she would look out the window. She did not like to see Mary, the Mother of Christ, outside her window.

The layers of separation were being laid on me. The most telling one was that when I was searching for a new job, she encouraged me to look at states that were distant from our home. She said that my father would do well enough without me. My father at the time was in his mid-80's and my only living relative. I was not about to leave my Dad by himself just so I could find the job of my dreams. It all came to a head when I was getting ready to be interviewed by a large monolithic pharmaceutical company in the big city close to where I lived. This coworker took it upon herself to lecture me about what and what not to do before the job interview. When the arrangements to go to visit for that face to face interview became firm, I had intended to take my Dad with me to stay with me in my hotel room so that I would feel safe away from home. I did not want to be alone in a hotel in downtown Indianapolis and my father himself would not feel happy knowing that he was miles and miles away from me.

This 'friend' had a meltdown when she heard that my Dad was coming with me. She warned me that this company would "know" that I planned to check in the hotel with my Dad. She insisted that this company would NOT hire me because Dad was a part of my life. She was so violently adamant that this company, any company like it, frowned on parents being a part of an employee's life. Parents were not to be seen nor heard from in this company, said this woman.

So back to the Separator thing. The woman I am speaking of was one element of the Separation Operation that the Evil one plays on every single child of God. It is all over the place, the culture and the US way of life. Everyone goes through this at some time in their life. The first step is when kids go off to college and their parents are suffering from empty nest syndrome. The next phase is when kids get a job far away from home, far from friends, far from support systems. This phase is the worst. It makes a person feel alone, terrified, and clinging to anyone that will give them a 'helping hand'. Nobody can be sure that that 'helping hand' is really good or bad. What is true is that FAMILY is good and friends can be bad. It is that phase where many Americans and maybe other westernized cultures get far away from God. There is no need to go to church anymore, no need to care about anyone at home, someone else will take care of the parents. Parents are left in their own homes feeling as though maybe they did something that they ought not have, and they get older before their time. Parents are left with latent illnesses aren't apparent because the kids aren't there frequently to detect them. Suddenly, the parents die or one is widowed and they don't last much after their spouse has gone. The children don't see how this is all part of the Evil One's work. Without that anchor of parents children have no recourse, no wise and sage advisor to guide them through life's problems.

I remember the Bible quotation (I'm rephrasing it here) about how God will bless the child who takes care of his parents. This is truth too. It is the most truthful thing because if children DON'T abandon their parents, then GOD WON'T ABANDON the children.

The Separation Operation must STOP. It must STOP with YOU. It must stop at all costs so that FAMILIES keep together. Where does it say that a job is THE most important thing in the life of a human being? A job is important, but there is more to it than that. If a job takes you away from your most important people in your life, then that job is Hell and is a bait by the Devil to separate you from God. Yes, from God. Because He is the ultimate Source of Your LIFE. He gave you your parents, your loved home, your dog and cat, your kids, your Church, your Faith, your very self and your SOUL. God will provide and you must always trust in His Divine Providence. So, when you start looking around in your life, and neighborhood for those who are Separators, ask yourself whether You have become one of the Devil's victims.

I really must say that listening to that priest was almost as though God Himself was TALKING to me. I didn't go to that church that often and only went on a whim to that parish that Sunday. I know now that God WAS talking to me at that point. It was as though He saw what was happening with me with my new friend, and He warned me through the words of that priest that I was about to become prey to the Separator. That Separator the Devil.

My thoughts for you are to listen and watch and ask God to speak to you and to recognize His Voice wherever He may talk to you. It is so very important. For those who don't think Families are great because of tensions or that misnomer "family discontent", this is not so. Families are not perfect, for sure, but families are what we are given. We must then strive to seek God in each of our family members. God dwells in them in one way or another. If there is anything that is not comfortable, look for the Separator in your midst to take the blame. God is everywhere. He is EVERYWHERE. He Sees all and Knows all. If you feel as though He is missing from your life, then count how many Separators are in your life now. I can guarantee you that you will be surprised to know that there are so many of them and they are fogging up the window to God.

www.ingramcontent.com/pod-product-compliance
Lightning Source LLC
Chambersburg PA
CBHW042050290426
44110CB00001B/9